TEST YOUR CHILD

GW01191738

Punctuation Practice

Frank Spooncer

Headway · Hodder & Stoughton

Notes for parents

Understanding and applying the rules of punctuation is a vital part of writing good English, which is a core subject of the National Curriculum, tested nationally from the age of seven.

This book aims to give your child plenty of practice in using punctuation correctly, while allowing you to assess any gaps he or she may have in her or her knowledge of punctuation.

Although there are some clear-cut 'rights and wrongs' in punctuation, there are also areas of choice. Where answers are given, these may still leave room for profitable discussion.

In general, the work becomes harder throughout the book. The first part tests knowledge of individual marks, while the later sections provide overall assessments of general ability to use punctuation correctly. No 'punctuation ages' are provided. Instead, an indication is given of how near your child has come to getting his or her 'punctuation licence'. The test section at the back can be used to assess both which parts of the book your child needs to work on, and to review his or her progress.

This Headway edition first published 1992

© 1992 Frank Spooncer

British Library Cataloguing-in-Publication data
Spooncer, Frank
   Punctuation practice. – (Test your child)
   I. Title   II. Series
   428.1

   ISBN 0-340-57044-X

Typeset by Litho Link Ltd., Welshpool, Powys

Printed in Great Britain for the educational
publishing division of Hodder & Stoughton Ltd,
Mill Road, Dunton Green, Sevenoaks, Kent, by
CW Print Group, Loughton, Essex.

Contents

Survey Section

The Punctuation Code 4
Capitals 5
Full stops 7
Full Stops and Abbreviations 8
Commas 9
Question Marks 10
Speech Marks 11
The Apostrophe 12
Speech Marks, Full Stops and Commas 14
A Mixture for You 15
Addresses and Letters 16

Story Section

Man Bites Dog 18
Poem Page 19
Corny Corner 20
Fillemin I 21
Fillemin II 22
Fillemin III 24
Excerpts to Punctuate 26

Test Section

Ones 27
Twos 29
Threes 30
Answers: Ones, Twos, Threes 31

I am grateful to the staff and pupils of Hillsgrove Primary School, Welling, Kent for their assistance in developing the material in this book.

The Punctuation Code

Before we can be safe on the roads, we need to know the Highway Code. This contains a set of signs. Some are to give advice, and some are to be obeyed.

The 'Punctuation Code' is something like that. It is a set of signs which help us to get the proper message from printed material. Without it, there would be as much confusion as there would be on the roads if all the signs were taken away. Although it may not seem as important as reading or spelling, good punctuation will improve your English. This book tests you on the Punctuation Code. If you can do it all correctly, you are certainly entitled to a full Punctuation Licence.

Before you begin, here is a little test on the signs to make sure you know them. Put the right sign in each of the boxes below.

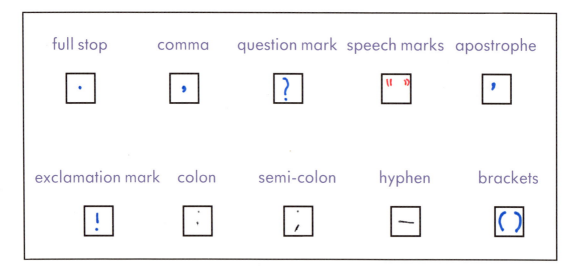

The exercises on the following pages include all of these signs, first one at a time and then in twos or threes. In the second part of the book are stories, rhymes and puzzles – and a test of your safety on the Punctuation Road.

Drive carefully!

Capitals

Some capitals have been left out of these sentences. Rewrite the sentences, putting CAPITALS in their proper places.

A1 come home from school early. aunt mary is coming to tea.

Come home from school early. Aunt Mary is coming to tea.

2 we went to spain last year. it was very hot every day.

We went to Spain last year. I was very hot every day.

3 our dog is called barker. he is very noisy.

Our dog is called Barker. He is very noisy.

4 there used to be 240 pennies in a pound. now there are 100 pence.

There used to be 240 pennies. ~~Now~~ in a pound .

5 keep this book until tomorrow. mrs white will collect it.

6 when i climbed mount snowdon, i could see for miles.

7 our club is called the rovers. we play every saturday.

8 mary is captain. i play in goal. our left back is pete.

Mary is captain. I play in goal. Our left back is Pete.

Write these names, putting capital letters where they should be. Try to match each name with the right place.

the prime minister   the house at pooh corner
winner the pooh   buckingham palace
queen elizabeth II   no. 10 downing street
president of the usa   hampton court palace
king henry VIII   the white house

vinney

Name:	Place:
B1 The Prime Minister	No.10 Downing Street
2 King Henry VIII	Hampton Court Palace
3 Winnie the Pooh	The house at Pooh Corner
4 Queen Elizabeth II	Buckingham Palace.
5 President of the U.S.A.	The White House.

5

Capitals

Here are some poems. Write them out, putting in capital letters where needed.

A

'bring in that pie,' said the fat little king.
'little miss muffet shall hear my birds sing.'

B

there once was a king – king canute –
who sat by the thames with a flute.
he said to duke willy,
'you may think i'm silly,
but i'll send the thames back with one toot.'

C

old ramble-by-night is a restless cat
who travels from scotland each day.
on the night express he speeds through the land
and you'll hear the passengers say,
'we all feel safe when ramble's aboard
as we roar through glasgow and perth,
and the villages – catfold and stretton-by-miaow –
rejoice with the sound of our mirth.'

Old ramble-by-night is a restless cat
Who travels from scotland each day.
On the night express he speeds though the land
and you'll hear the passengers say
we all feel safe when ramble's aboard
as we roar through glasgow and perth
and the villages - catfold and stretton-by-miaow
rejoice with the sound of our mirth.

6

Full Stops

Some breathless person has been chattering away, so there are no full stops in the sentenced below. Remember also to put CAPITAL LETTERS in the proper places when you write the sentences correctly.

A Billy went into the garden.the door of the hutch was open.he looked inside. the rabbit was gone.he sat down and cried.

_____

_____

_____

B Mary got on the horse.the crowd was silent.she rode towards the high wall. up horse and rider flew.they were over.the crowd cheered.the cup was hers.

_____

_____

_____

C The storm waves crashed onto the ark.lightning flashed and thunder roared.the animals brayed and squealed for seven days.the gales blew.the end came with a rainbow in the sky.

_____

_____

_____

This story also needs capital letters and full stops. Some of the capitals are _not_ after the full stops.

D king arthur had a magician called merlin.merlin gave arthur a flying horse called skyflier.arthur flew it to his court at camelot before breakfast every day except sunday.

_____

_____

_____

Full Stops and Abbreviations

With a title like 'Dr' for 'Doctor' or 'Mr' for 'Mister', the letters are missing from the *middle* of the word. In that case, there is no full stop. There *is* a full stop when letters are missing from the end (e.g. 'Prof.' for 'Professor'). These ladies and gentlemen have some full stops missing from their titles. Write the correct form on the lines beneath.

A1   J M Foster

    J. M. Foster

  2   Mrs C D Westerley

  3   P T Cudliffe, Esq

4   Dr L N Suchman, M R C P

5   Prof H T Vanderton

6   The Rt Hon A St J Evans, M P

These poor people have lost their capials as well as their full stops. Please help them.

B1   mr j n stephens

    Mr. J. N. Stephens

  2   the very revd dr turnbull

  3   r t ridgers, esq

4   h r h princess of wales

5   col d c cooke-evans, d s o

6   ms c o frederick, l r a m

These folk would be grateful if you could shorten their long titles. Put in capitals and full stops.

C1   doctor ivor llewellyn lloyd rees-davies, member of the royal college of surgeons

    Dr. I. L. L. Rees-Davies, M. R. C. S

  2   mister jonathan william leavem-alone, member of the royal society for the protection of birds

Commas

This is a saying to help you remember the number of days in each month. Write in the four correct months, and add commas where they are needed.

A   Thirty days hath _____

_____

Put commas in the proper places in these sentences:

B1   This year I sold 2796 spades 3658 forks and about 1000000 spring bulbs.

2   In the year 1985 there were over 56000000 men women and children in Britain. Many families owned cars a few had private planes or helicopters but none had their own spacecraft or rocket. Will this change by the year 2000?

These sentences read rather strangely at the moment. Rewrite them, putting the commas in the proper places.

C1   Waiting in the icy cold for the bus the lady wanted a cup of hot tea scones jam and butter.

2   It really doesn't matter if I don't get any fatter and I don't get any fatter what I do.
(*Winnie the Pooh*).

These sentences have commas in the wrong places. Rewrite the sentences, using commas to make the meaning clear.

D1   John entered the room on his head, a hat on his feet,

_____

Wellingtons on his hands, gloves.

_____

2   Mum ate Charles, drank some wine, and Dad, finished with a

_____

black coffee.

_____

Question Marks

Some of the sentences below need question marks, but some do not. Write 'Yes' in the answer column if a question mark is needed, 'No' if it isn't.

Question Mark?

A1   Are you Welsh   *Yes*

  2   The lady asked if I was Welsh   *No*

  3   The lady asked, 'Are you Welsh'   *Yes*

  4   You are Welsh, aren't you   *Yes*

Some of these sentences have question marks in the wrong places, some have question marks left out, and some shouldn't have any at all. Write out the sentences using the right punctuation.

B1   The Prime Minister demanded an answer to the question?

_____

  2   You jumped 2 metres! I don't believe it?

_____

  3   Do you expect me to believe that you jumped 2 metres?

_____

  4   The Space Commander asked why the Task Fleet wasn't ready?   *With or without a question M*

_____

  5   'Will you walk a little faster?' said the Whiting to the Snail?

_____

_____

Put question marks and full stops in the right places in this silly conversation:

C1   Mr. A: Why have you got a carrot in your ear ?

_____

  2   Mr. B: It scares tigers, doesn't it

_____

  3   Mr. A: How do you know. There aren't any around here are there ?

_____

  4   Mr. B: Why should there be? My carrot has scared them away.

_____

Speech Marks

'Well done!'

Punctuate this little story, using speech marks around the actual words used. All the other punctuation marks have been put in for you.

A   The Space Controller dropped the Galaxy Directory on his foot. 'Blast it,' he cried. 'Right, Sir,' said the Mission Officer. 'Blasting off now.' Who did that?' cried a voice from 50,000 feet.

Now do the same for this family argument:

B   'The next train goes at three o'clock,' said Dad.
Mum cried, upset, 'We'll never make it.'
'Let's take a taxi,' suggested Dick. 'That will do the trick.'
'It's your fault, Dick,' Mary shouted, 'because you spent so long packing your silly toys. You can pay the fare.'

Tom and Jerry are at war again. Punctuate this poem using speech marks to show what they actually said.

C
        'I feel merry,' said Jerry.
        'How come?' asked Tom.
        'I'm a mouse in a house,
        Far too old to get cold.'
        'We'll see about that,'
        Said Tom, the fat cat.

Here are some examples of 'reported speech'. Change each sentence writing it out to show the exact words that were said. Put in speech marks where necessary. Be careful with the <u>tense</u> (past, present . . .) that you use.

D   The captain said that they must win their next match. Ten losses in a row were ten too many. '

_____

_____

The angry goalkeeper said that it wasn't all his fault. The week before, he let in only eight goals.'

_____

_____

_____

The Apostrophe

An apostrophe can be used to show something or someone belongs to something or someone else.

A1   the son of the king _the king's son_

  2   the king of the people _____

  3   the people of the king _____

  4   the new clothes of the Emperor _____

  5   the feet of the giants _____

  6   the fans of the princesses _____

  7   the bleating of the sheep _____

  8   the cries of the freezing lamb _____

An apostrophe may show words are shortened, with something left out.
Write the short form of these phrases, using the apostrophe:

B1   that is right _that's right_   5   I have not _____

  2   he cannot _____   5   who is there? _____

  3   we should not _____   7   he had gone _____

  4   it is raining _____   8   they will not _____

Write out these phrases, without using the apostrophe.

C1   they've gone away _they have gone away_

  2   we're coming now _____

  3   Jack's arrived already _____

  4   Mary's arriving today _____

  5   you mustn't tell lies _____

  6   the queen's crown _the crown of the queen_

  7   the hive's queen _____

  8   the doctors' surgeries _____

  9   the doctor's prescriptions _____

The Apostrophe

All of these sentences, have at *least* one mistake. Write the sentences correctly on the lines below, using apostrophes in the right way.

A1   The ladies shoe's aren't ready yet.

_____

2   I'll make sure theyr'e ready tomorrow.

_____

3   Its' cold out there. Won't you come in?.

_____

4   The weathers' awful, but I shouldn't stay long. I'm late now.

_____

_____

5   The new Emperors' clothes aren't nearly as fine as his father's.

_____

_____

Careful with this one! Some of the apostrophes are in the wrong place, some are missed out – and some shouldn't be there at all! Write the correct sentences on the lines.

B
The policemen's car stopped at the clubs door.

_____

'Wev'e had complaints' about noise,' said one policeman.

_____

'Sorry, officers,' replied the owner. 'It's our twin son's

_____

21st birthdays' and we're having a party. The policeman

_____

answered 'Your'e disturbing your next door neighbour's childrens' sleep.

_____

Parties are nice, but you keep yours' quieter, won't you?'

_____

Speech Marks, Full Stops and Commas

In this first set, the speech marks and commas are missing. Put them in very clearly where you think they belong. You may find it easier to write the sentences out again on a separate piece of paper.

A1 Long John Silver cried, Shiver my timbers shiver my timbers.

2 The parrot replied Pieces of eight pieces of eight.

3 The rain in Spain said Eliza falls mainly in the plain.

4 In Hereford Hertford and Huntingdon she went on hurricanes hardly ever 'appen.

5 You can't be serious said the tennis player to the umpire. That ball was in. In your mind it was in not in mine said the umpire. One more in like that and you're out.

Commas, full stops and speech marks are missing here.

B1 Tell me the words he used ordered the Judge

2 The witness replied that he said You are the silliest son of a sausage I ever saw

Here is a conversation from the planet Esrever, where, of course, everything is said in reverse, or *backwards*. Write out the conversation, punctuated in Earthman's style.

C   htrae morf enoyna tem reve uoy evah asked the esrevan

'Have you ever met anyone from Earth?' asked the esrevan

on replied his friend meht tuoba tahw

_____

Idnatsrednu yllaer t'nod i said the esrevan yas yeht drow a

_____

sdrawkcab kaeps yehT

_____

A Mixture for You

This page tests how well you can use the COLON (:), the SEMI-COLON (;), the HYPHEN (-) and BRACKETS ().

Use the COLON to introduce these lists.

A1 Pupils must bring the following to their examination pencils, graph paper and drawing instruments.
  2 The British Isles England, Scotland, Wales, Northern Ireland and the Irish Republic.

Use the SEMI-COLON to divide these sentences.

B1 The bell rang the children cheered the teacher smiled the term was over.
  2 The shot rang out the villain fell justice had been done.
  3 Jack left Meg left Sue left in the end there was only me.

Use the HYPHEN where it is used to link words.

C1 Can a son in law be married to a daughter in law?
  2 The second hand has just fallen off my third hand watch.
  3 The long winded speech of the vice president was very boring, even to his well wishers.

Use the EXCLAMATION MARK where it would be good for emphasis.

D1 Bring that bone here, Muncher It's our leg of lamb
  2 Load Aim Fire
  3 Good heavens Could a camel possibly wear that coat?

Put BRACKETS where you think they are needed to set words apart.

E1 Racket games tennis, squash, badminton require a lot of skill.
  2 The hero Dr Ponsonby was very forceful, but the gardener Fred Jardine seemed uneasy.

Use marks shown on this page for the next item.

F Rubbish If you had co operated like Mabel we would never have gone to Wetter on Sea. This is what it cost me twenty pounds in fares a day's work two thousand grey hairs and my best hat, stolen by a hungry sea gull.

Addresses and Letters

Here are some addresses which the postman would find rather hard to sort out. Write them out as they should be.

A1   a tenor   7A opera ct chorus lane warbleshire

          A. Tenor

2   dr i mendem fracture clinic curemall hospital stretcher rd wheelemin

Here is a letter which seems to have been written by a puppy who can't punctuate properly. Help his uncle get the message by rewriting the letter with capital letters and the proper marks. Use a separate piece of paper.

3 terrier ct
dalmatian rd
woofingham
barkshire

dear uncle spot

i hope you're well and wagging your tail as strongly as ever we're all fit here

i've been entering competitions with tom we have to jump fences climb ladders and go through tunnels at least i have to while tom shows me the way

we went to howlbury grange yesterday there were terriers alsatians retrievers and several other rather mixed up dogs tom and i beat them all and the president gave us a cup

mum dad tom and i will come over to wagtail bay to see you soon and well bring the cup with us

your affectionate nephew

tiny the terrier

Letters II

Here is a letter from a very disappointed customer, complaining to the presenter of a well-known TV programme. Rewrite the letter on a separate piece of paper. Punctuate it correctly so that Esther can understand it.

esther rantzen   7 naggers court
thats life   complaints rd
bbc   grumbledum GB1 4H
shepherds bush
london w11

dear esther rantzen

a week ago on the 10 january i bought a radio controlled model car called the magician from the following traders

i konyu
profit house
rookem LP1 2EH

the description said it would i quote

obey your every command turn circles reverse do wheelies climb hills and turbo boost

so far it has

1   tripped up dad smashing his best pipe
2   turbo boosted itself through the china cabinets window
3   steered itself into the high st causing a five car pile up

i think youll agree thats not good for five days so called obedience to commands id be glad to show the magicians abilities or rather lack of them on your programme should you be prepared to risk it

yours sincerely

i monalot

Speech Marks

This rather strange story needs speech marks. Put them in *very clearly* where you think they belong.

MAN BITES DOG

A man came up to a dog in the street. The man shouted take that, biting the dog right on the nose.

The dog wailed, woo-woo-woo, and ran to its mistress.

Why are you biting my dog? she cried.

Just then a policeman came up, asking about all the fuss.

I'll see him in court, roared the lady, for biting my Peterkins.

Did you actually *see* him bite the dog? the policeman enquired.

Of course, said the lady, and so did my Peterkins.

You'll woof to that in court, won't you, darling?

Woof, woof, barked the dog.

The man admitted in court that he did bite the dog.

Then you must pay a fine, ordered the judge.

The man asked how he could pay a fine.

I haven't any money, he explained.

The judge looked over his glasses at the man, saying,

Are you telling me that you have no money for food?

He went on. Were you going to *eat* the dog for your lunch?

Of course not, said the man, shaking his head.

He paused. But if I hadn't bitten the dog, I'm sure he would have bitten me.

Poem Page

Here are some poems for you to punctuate. Write out the poems on a separate paper.

THE DOVER ROAD

they rode the road to dover
sir harry prince and he
from marble arch they started
by tyburns ancient tree
through canterbury their horses swept
the watchmen cried ho there
but none could stop the flying hooves
of the brave young english pair

LADY PROPOSES, MAN REFUSES!

will you will you billy
will you marry me
no my little mary
i won't marry thee
why oh why my billy
arent i good enough for thee
no oh no my mary
youre much too good for me

This one may cause some arguments – and show you the importance of correct punctuation.

DRAKE BOWLS OUT ARMADA

queen elizabeth asked sir francis drake
tell me how long do you think it would take
to singe the king of spains new beard
as long as a game of bowls thats what i feared

Corny Corner

Put in the proper punctuation marks where there is a dash, and change small letters to CAPITALS where they are needed.

A
PETER: Please _ miss _ does ham grow like a plant _
TEACHER: no _ it most certainly doesn _ t _
PETER: then what_s _ an ambush _ miss _

B
SIR: michael _ what _ s the order of the bath _
MICHAEL: well _ sir _ it _ s usually may first _ margaret _ second _ molly third _ and then me _

C
TEACHER: alastair _ make up a sentence which contains the word_ gruesome _ _
PUPIL: dad put fertilizer on our little puppy _ and now it _ s sure gruesome _

D
PASSENGER: where is this train going to _ porter _
PORTER: that train goes to plymouth in five minutes _ madam _
PASSENGER: amazing _ what progress _ the last time i went to devon _ it took at least three hours _

E
LADY: who are you _
MAN AT DOOR: i _ m the piano _ tuner _ madam _
LADY: i never asked a piano _ tuner to call _ did i _
MAN: no _ lady _ but your neighbours did _

F
The boring singer in the albert hall said _ _ i_d now like to sing _ over the hills and far away _ _ _
_ thank goodness for that _ _ whispered a member of the audience _ i thought he was here for the night _ _

Fillemin I

This is called a 'Fillemin' because there are some gaps for punctuation marks. You have to fill 'em in!
Remember to change small letters to CAPITALS where you think they are needed.

MRS CABBAGE PATCH AND THE COMPUTER

it was getting near christmas _ mrs cabbage patch was at her wits _ end _
_ whatever can i get that cabbage kid _ _ she asked herself _
_ christmas morning will come on the old patch _ and there _ ll be nothing for her _ she _ ll water the caulis with her cabbage tears _ _
just as she was huffing and puffing along the high street _ she saw a notice in a shop window _

KOMPUTERS FOR KIDS

it said _
_ the very thing _ _ she thought _ _ I don _ t understand these things _ but crafty carol will work it out in a flash _ so on christmas morning there was a large parcel addressed to carol beside the christmas cabbage _ mrs c _ p _ had taken a lot of trouble over the cabbage _ It looked really colourful decorated with carrots _ parsnips and radishes though the smell was rather strong _ after a very quick rustling and tearing of paper _ there was a cry from carol _ _ a computer and software _
_ here I go _ _ said carol _ _ you _ re not going to believe what i _ ll do with this _ first _ a _ thank you _ to mum _ _ this is what came out _

CARol's cristMAS *Thank* You

_ oh well _ _ said carol _ _ even computers make mistakes _ _

Fillemin II

Once more, you have to fill in the right marks where there is a dash, and change small letters to CAPITALS where they are needed.

THE STRANGE WHITE BEAST

Andrew had left his house early to go for a walk in the forest _ he found he had wandered into a green _ carpeted clearing _ he listened _ was that a sound _ yes _ there was a slight rustling in the bushes _ a white form appeared _

first a nose pushed out _ then two shining blue eyes looked down on andrew _ what was it _ he waited _ was it a horse _ would it come out _ was it dangerous _ he stepped back a little _

_ creature _ _ said andrew _ _ you are real _ the animal came out further _ one step _ two steps _ into the deep green grass _

_ you are a horse _ aren't you _ he asked again _ it was true _ but had there ever been so sleek _ so white a coat on any other horse _ had there ever been eyes so bright _ so intelligent _ had there ever been so beautiful a creature _

_ my name is andrew _ _ he said _ _ what is yours _ _ the animal looked straight at him _ it did not seem to speak _ but andrew was sure he heard _ in clear and musical tones he said _ _ my name is pegasus _ _

22

_ then you must be able to fly _ _ said andrew _ who knew the Greek story _

_ not exactly fly _ _ replied pegasus _ _ but if you climb on my back _ i can take you anywhere you like in space and time _ where would you like to go _ _

_ i would like to see myself thirty years from now _ said andrew _
_ very well _ so you shall _ climb on my back _ close your eyes _ and hold on _ _

there was a gentle sort of rushing sound _ a soft warm breeze _ and a pleasant swaying motion _

_ you may open your eyes now _ _ said the horse _
andrew did so _ _ you _ ve cheated me _ _ he said _ _ everything _ s the same as before _ _

_ wait a moment _ _ said pegasus _
they waited _ and soon a small boy _ very much like andrew _ came into the clearing _ he stopped and listened _ _ that can _ t be me _ _ said andrew _ _
i_m here _ not'there _ _ _ it_s your son _ _ said pegasus _ _ watch _ _
they watched _ there was a slight rustling in the bushes _ a white form appeared . . .

Fillemin III

Once more, you fill in the marks where there is a dash, and change any small letters to CAPITALS where they are needed.

The Island of Sighs

_ when are we starting _ _ asked sarah _ _ the jones _ s boat has left already _ _ _ we_ll be off soon _ _ said her father _ _ we_ve been held up by mum _ she_s packed ices _ spices _ all things niceys for lunch _ she wouldn_t let us go without them _ _ sarah turned to mum _ _ that_s all very well _ _ she said _ _but i_d like to eat before the sun goes down_ _

_ cast off _ _ roared dad _ and they were away _ a fresh breeze fanned the sails _ gentle ripples rocked the hull _ the land faded further and further away _ _ this is heaven _ _ exclaimed mr smith _ leaning by the rudder _ not quite _ _ replied david _ _ it _ s called _ the island of sighs _ _ _

_ that_s an odd name _ _ said mum _ _ why is it called that _ _

dad explained that everyone is sad when they leave _ and so they sigh _

_ hurry up _ then _ _ said sarah _ _ it sounds wonderful _ _

_ avast there _ ye lubbers _ _ roared a voice _

_ oh no _ _ moaned david _ _ not him again _ _

over the top of the hill appeared the three _ cornered hat of short jack gold _ otherwise known as the revd john pulpit _ from st george _ s _

he had organised everything every well _ first _ the children were divided into
pirates and seafarers _ given a map _ and sent to search for hidden clues such
as _

_ take fifteen strides from the highest tides _

then search beneath the stricken birch _ _

each clue kept them running here and there _ up and down _ in and out _
sometimes they had to work in groups _ perhaps crossing a wide stream with
the help of the ropes _ wood and tools provided _ they weren _ t allowed to do
anything silly _ like pushing a pirate into a pond _ parents stood by the clues to
see all was fair _ david and sarah were pirates _ after a close race round the
island _ they were the first to reach a thin _ tattered old scroll _ this is what it
said _

_ climb _ it seems _ a thousand stairs _

there amongst the windy airs _

high above the ocean blue _

you _ ll find concealed the final chew _ _

_ they mean the final clue _ not the final chew _ don_t
they _ _ said david _ placing it back under the moss _ covered rock _
they gazed around _ _ the lighthouse _ _ cried sarah _ they raced up the
winding stairs _ at the top were two chests _ one labelled _ pirates _ _ the other,
_ seafarers _ _ they opened one _ it was packed full of sweets and chocolates
_ it did mean the final chew after all _ _ said david _
_ three cheers for short jack gold _ _

Excerpts

Here are some passages from books for children. Rewrite them on a separate paper as you think they would appear in the books.

A.   nana was busy putting the children to bed she began as usual with michael she had put on his bath taken the towel in her mouth and set michael on her back to carry him but michael was cross because he couldnt stay up any longer he shouted and kicked and said he wasnt going to bed i wont i wont he cried and i dont love you any more nana

(From *Peter Pan and Wendy* by J.M. Barrie, published by Hodder and Stoughton)

B.   so they went into the tea room and there was the birthday tea spread out on the table bad harrys mother had made red jellies and yellow jellies and blancmanges and biscuits and sandwiches and cakes with cherries on and a big birthday cake white icing on it and candles and happy birthday harry written on it
     my naughty little sisters eyes grew bigger and bad harry said theres something else in the larder its going to be a surprise treat but you shall see it because you are my best girl friend

(From the collection *Stories for Children*, edited by Anne Wood, published by Hodder and Stoughton)

C.   a little man opened the door tipped his hat and said good evening millers daughter why is it that you weep so the king has ordered me to spin straw into gold and i dont know how she answered him and began to weep again the little man squinted up his eyes and said what will you give me if i spin it for you i have very little to give said the millers daughter but there is my necklace

(From *The Illustrated Treasury of Fairy Tales*, edited by T.A. Kennedy, published by Hodder and Stoughton)

Ones, Twos and Threes

Ones

In these exercises you only need *one* kind of punctuation mark. The one you need is shown at the top. Draw a ring round any marks you put in.

In Set A you need FULLSTOPS (.)

A1   This is the man I saw yesterday
 2   This is the man I saw him yesterday
 3   This is the man I saw him He ran away
 4   Peter is a boy Mary is a girl Spot is a dog

In set B you need COMMAS (,)

B1   Flies can't bird but birds can fly.
 2   The army had 250000 foot soldiers 12000 horsemen 1750 field guns and still lost the battle.
 3   I'll have a portion of chips three sausages two large cod and a steak and kidney pie.
 4   James who wasn't hungry gave all his chips away.

In set C you need SPEECH MARKS (' ')

C1   James' sister asked, Aren't you hungry?
 2   Don't eat that, said Mum. It's stone cold.
 3   It's cold, replied Mary, because you talk so much.
 4   But you said I mustn't talk with my mouth full, said James.

In Set D you need QUESTION MARKS (?)

D1   Are whales fish or not
 2   Is a Lotus a flower or a bird Is a Cavalier a horseman
 3   The old lady asked, 'Will you help me across the road'
 4   'Are you going far' asked the boy.

In Set E you need APOSTROPHES (')

E1   It's not the colour weve been expecting. Youll have to change it, wont you?
 2   The Kings regiment lined up in St Georges Square to receive its new flag from the Colonels hand.
 3   The childrens teachers told the youngsters mothers where each childs peg was.
 4   Youre sure your books are in Susans desk, arent you?

In this section, you need CAPITALS. Show where they belong by rewriting the sentences.

F1 the duke of buccleugh wrote a book called *how to live in a railway truck.*

_____

2 i was told by dr foster of gloucester that i should go to worcester for

_____

my booster.

_____

3 'don't eat bread,' james lead said. 'it's a great mistake.

_____

eat dundee cake.'

_____

Twos

In Set A you need CAPITALS and FULL STOPS.

A1 peter said to wendy, 'you and i will go high into the sky where shall

_____

we fly?'

_____

2 i shall go first to secondton after that i will visit j p thirdum of fourthville

_____

finally, i'll return to lastown

_____

In Set B you need CAPITALS and SPEECH MARKS.

B1 mr asker asked his class,

_____

did you ask about your maths?

_____

yes, i did, young john replied.

_____

my dad told me i must divide.

_____

2   mr andrews said, apple.   banana, said dr burton.

lady colt said, cherry.   pass, said king zachariah.

In set C you need QUESTION MARKS and APOSTROPHES.

C1   Is this Janes Is this Marys Whose is that

2   If it isn't yours youll have to give it back, wont you

3   Its strange that their shields are like ours, isnt it

4   Theyre not so strong, though, are they

In set D you need COMMAS and QUESTION MARKS.

D1   Is a whale a fish an animal a monster or a mammal

2   James asked 'Who wants a sausage Who wants chips Who wants peas'

3   'Can't you see me' asked Tom 'standing so high up here'

Threes

For Set A you need CAPITALS, FULL STOPS and COMMAS. Write the correct sentences on the below.

A1   peter piper picked a peck of pickled peppers peaches plums and popadums

2   the centre forward bill richards saw his chance he rose high headed and

the game was won

3   the train for bath leaves at 11 a m sir it calls at reading swindon and bath

arriving at 12 47 p m

For Set B you need COMMAS, QUESTION MARKS, and SPEECH MARKS.

B1   What did you see children when you went to the Zoo asked the teacher.

_____

I saw lions tigers and crocodiles didn't I said little Tony.

_____

2   May I have a sandwich with peanut butter cheese and pickles Sue asked

_____

her Mum.

_____

With or without stomach-ache Mum enquired reaching for the bread bin.

_____

For Set C you need COMMAS, APOSTROPHES, and SPEECH MARKS.

C1   Bills safe said Mr Thornton thankfully. Hes been rescued from the cliff.

_____

2   Thats Johns bike James cried Mother. Dont play with other childrens toys

_____

without asking first.

_____

In this last set you need SPEECH MARKS, QUESTION MARKS
and CAPITALS.

D1   PASSENGER   PORTER

where can i get a train for ware   where, sir

_____

ware.   ah, ware. over there.

_____

ANSWERS: Ones, Twos, Threes

There is a point for each punctuation mark correctly added, and for each correct change from a small to a capital letter.

Ones

A1   This is the man I saw yesterday.
  2   This is the man. I saw him yesterday.
  3   This is the man. I saw him. He ran away.
  4   Peter is a boy. Mary is a girl. Spot is a dog.

B1   Flies can't bird, but birds can fly.
  2   The army had 250,000 foot soldiers, 12,000 horsemen, 1,750 field guns and still lost the battle.
  3   I'll have a portion of chips, three sausages, two large cod and a steak and kidney pie.
  4   James, who wasn't hungry, gave all his chips away.

C1   James' sister asked, 'Aren't you hungry?'
  2   'Don't eat that,' said Mum. 'It's stone cold.'
  3   'It's cold,' replied Mary, 'because you talk so much.'
  4   'But you said I mustn't talk with my mouth full,' said James.

D1   Are whales fish or not?
  2   Is a Lotus a flower or a bird? Is a Cavalier a horseman?
  3   The old lady asked, 'Will you help me across the road?'
  4   'Are you going far?' asked the boy.

E1   It's not the colour we've been expecting. You'll have to change it, won't you?
  2   The King's regiment lined up in St George's Square to receive its new flag from the Colonel's hand.
  3   The children's teachers told the youngsters' mothers where each child's peg was.
  4   You're sure your books are in Susan's desk, aren't you?

F1   The Duke of Buccleugh wrote a book called *How to live in a railway truck*.
  2   I was told by Dr Foster of Gloucester that I should go to Worcester for my booster.
  3   'Don't eat bread,' James Lead said. 'It's a great mistake. Eat Dundee cake.'

Twos

A1   Peter said to Wendy, 'You and I will go high into the sky. Where shall we fly?'
  2   I shall go first to Secondton. After that I will visit J.P. Thirdum at Fourthville. Finally, I'll return to Lastown.

B1   Mr Asker asked his class,
      'Did you ask about your maths?'
      'Yes, I did,' young John replied.
      'My dad told me I must divide.'
  2   Mr Andrews said, 'Apple.' 'Banana,' said Dr Burton. Lady Colt said, 'Cherry.' 'Pass,' said King Zachariah.

C1 Is that Jane's? Is this Mary's? Whose is that?

  2 If it isn't yours you'll have to give it back, won't you?

  3 It's strange that their shields are like ours, isn't it?

  4 They're not so strong, though, are they?

D1 Is a whale a fish, an animal, a monster or a mammal?

  2 James asked, 'Who wants a sausage? Who wants chips? Who wants peas?'

  3 'Can't you see me,' asked Tom, 'standing so high up here?'

Threes

A1 Peter Piper picked a peck of pickled peppers, peaches, plums and popadums.

  2 The centre forward, Bill Richards, saw his chance. He rose high, headed, and the game was won.

  3 The train for Bath leaves at 11 a.m., sir. It calls at Reading, Swindon and Bath, arriving at 12.47 p.m.

B1 'What did you see, children, when you went to the Zoo?' asked the teacher.
'I saw lions, tigers and crocodiles, didn't I?' said little Tony.

  2 'May I have a sandwich with peanut butter, cheese and pickles?' Sue asked her Mum.
'With or without stomach-ache?' Mum enquired, reaching for the bread bin.

C1 'Bill's safe,' said Mr Thornton thankfully.
'He's been rescued from the cliff.'

  2 'That's John's bike, James,' cried Mother. 'Don't play with other children's toys without asking first.'

D1 PASSENGER   PORTER
      'Where can I get a train for Ware?'   'Where, sir?
      'Ware.'   'Ah, Ware. Over there.'

Scoring for punctuation licence

Below 100 : Still early days. You need plenty of practice and some help from a qualified instructor.

100-149 : You have learned many of the basic rules. Keep practising and have some help on your weak points.

150-174 : You earn a Provisional Punctuation Licence. There are still some rules you need to learn before you gain a Full Licence.

175-199 : You deserve a Full Punctuation Licence. Your signals are now quite clear. Some extra attention to the more difficult rules and you'll be ready to try for an Advanced Licence.

Over 200 : Well done! You're an Advanced Punctuator.